ENTERING
ANOTHER COUNTRY

ENTERING ANOTHER COUNTRY

by

TONI ORTNER

All rights reserved, including without limitation the right to reproduce this book or any portion thereof in any form or by any means, whether electronic or mechanical, now known or hereinafter invented, without the express written permission of the publisher.

This is a work of fiction. Names, characters, places, events, and incidents either are the product of the author's imagination or are used fictitiously. Any resemblance to actual persons, living or dead, businesses, companies, events, or locales is entirely coincidental.

Originally published by The Basilisk Press.

Copyright © 1976, 2006 by Toni Ortner

ISBN: 978-1-5040-2923-0

Distributed in 2016 by Open Road Distribution
180 Maiden Lane
New York, NY 10038
www.openroadmedia.com

For My Mother and Father

CONTENTS

Here, at the Edge of the Land   1

Courage Is Like Perhaps   2

Where Would We Walk   3

Alma Mater   4

Let Love   5

The Wind that Fell Before the First Snow Came   6

Coney Island   7

How Hard I Tried to Reach You
    My Lithe Little Blond Sister   8

Poem for Eli Bodi Enzer   11

St. Michael's Cemetery   14

The Red Death Is Always a Surprise   16

All Along the Hudson the Boats Toot Tonight   17

Night Journey   18

Birth   19

Afternoon at the Zoo   20

Homage to Kandinsky   21

Tribute to Arshile Gorky   23

Note to Noah from His Wife   25

The Science Lesson   27

The High Wire Specialists   29

Still Life Artist   31

The Photograph   33

The Wednesday Ladies   35

At the Edge of the Desert   36

Entering Another Country   37

Rendezvous   43

The House in the Woods   46

Letting Go   50

Here They Come the Marching Drums   51

Lesson of the Horn in G   53

Themes Written Under Stress   54

River Poem   58

The Simple Things   61

ACKNOWLEDGMENTS

"Here, at the Edge of the Land," *KANSAS QUARTERLY*
"Courage Is Like Perhaps," *KANSAS QUARTERLY*
"Where Would We Walk," *CARDINAL POETRY QUARTERLY*
"Let Love," *LAUREL REVIEW*
"The Wind that Fell Before the First Snow Came," *FLORIDA QUARTERLY*
"Coney Island," *KANSAS QUARTERLY*
"Poem for Eli Bodi Enzer," *POET LORE & NEW ENGLAND REVIEW*
"St. Michael's Cemetery," *THE LITERARY REVIEW*
"The Red Death Is Always a Surprise," *FLORIDA QUARTERLY*
"All Along the Hudson the Boats Toot Tonight," *VOICES INTERNATIONAL*
"Night Journey," *CARDINAL POETRY QUARTERLY*
"Birth," *NEW ENGLAND REVIEW*
"Homage to Kandinsky," *CANADIAN FORUM*
"Tribute to Arshile Gorky," *FIDDLEHEAD*
"Note to Noah from His Wife," *CANADIAN FORUM*
"The Science Lesson," *KANSAS QUARTERLY*
"Alma Mater," *ROANOKE REVIEW*
"How Hard I Tried to Reach You My Lithe Little Blond Sister,"
    NEW ENGLAND REVIEW
"The Wednesday Ladies," *POEMS BY POETS (SOUTH AND WEST)*
"The House in the Woods," *CONNECTIONS*
"River Poem," *CONNECTIONS*
"The Simple Things," *CONNECTIONS*

ENTERING ANOTHER COUNTRY

HERE, AT THE EDGE OF THE LAND

Here, at the edge of the land
the earth suddenly pitches forward
strains and slips with a silent gasp
sideways under the sea;
but the cry of the seagull
the roar of the breakers rolling inwards
drown her surrender
in sweet disorder.
The brown seagrass flutters
like a woman's silky hair;
the pounding of wind
through her limbs
has made her pliant
and she bends like a lord
of her own accord
survives the surf
to shelter the wandering gull
from abroad
which swoops down slow
on heavy wing.
Here, at the edge of the land,
we had to come this far
to see again the stars
and feel the wet sand;
the Big Dipper rides
topsy-turvy above us,
the still bay water, inland, resounds
with the dank and starry skelter
of fishermen clanking chords
on rusty iron midnight riggings.

COURAGE IS LIKE PERHAPS

Courage is something
like perhaps
a gray elephant
a great gray elephant
who is what he is
all that weight
and nothing to do but push on
across the desert
and sand being what it is
so soft
and his weight still being his weight
there's nothing to do but plod on
each step he sinks
steps again
lifts each individual foot
unrhythmical, arduous
without applause
not like the circus
the large toes and flabby wrinkled flesh
the soft gray ears flapping wildly
dripping sweat
night falls
the moon
an icy sliver
he shivers and squints
as if perhaps he were looking into the future towards
some possible oasis
but
it is nothing
not even that
he is merely tired
too tired to even bother to count
the steps.

WHERE WOULD WE WALK

Just picking
the most appropriate
place of rendezvous
took an hour
the focal point
being far more
than one of foreground or background
this, in itself, indicative
and I no painter.

Where would we walk as we once did,
effortless, all half things whole
              understood?
At the ocean, perhaps, if anywhere
trimmed down to size like specks
on the rim of that giant heaving shore
if we should talk
the waters would murmur assent
but in our silence
we would be magnified
the waters
rush to engulf
the few words thrust,
futile as skimming stones
cast from the shore.

ALMA MATER

From my window
I watch the children running
running towards the stone lions on the marble steps
their shouts interspersed with laughter.
The professors walk past oblivious
briefcases jammed with *the facts*
intent upon the lesson to prepare
already formulating tomorrow's lecture.
The children
see things magic where we all once did
the grounds to them are geometric squares
greens, browns
not space to traverse.
For them, it's always spring in winter
and no sense of seasons past.
At dusk the white lamps glow
floating white balloons suspended in the clear sharp air.
Soon it will snow.
Age ends expectation
buries life with marble steps and schedules.
Children know better.
The eagle perched above the flag which rides at half mast
is not a symbol yet of country or death
it's still a shining golden bird
about to fly.
The evenings echo with the children's
laughter.

LET LOVE

The intellect
is a fox at bay
now
let Love slaughter it!

She has waited long
lean and silent
in her kennel of hunger.

God
Your Patience is too infinite for my taste.
Your Silence
Annihilates.

It is possible for me to go
and in my going hold you whole.
This, the last lie,
I clutch like a sheet
to shield me
from the razor eyes of morning.

"Just because you want
to believe a thing is true
doesn't make it so," you said.
"You won't remember anything once you're dead."

Can't I make you see how it is!
Alone with no horizon
the sun is lost;
a miniature balloon floating up and away.
A clenched fist
can't shut out the night
but an open palm gathers light
and That is Love.

These are only words to you.
I am through with metaphors.
I stuff them in a box and slam the lid.
My sky is streaked with blood.

THE WIND THAT FELL BEFORE THE FIRST SNOW CAME

The wind that fell before the first snow came said
the sun that nurses the apple's seed
engenders the worm that rots the core
have patience, you too grow old
shall blow away with me in time
into a kingdom beyond the night
where the clouds are golden
and the moon shines cold and bright
there all seasons are the same
now regard all with an equaniminous eye
and form no judgments
in the stillness of high noon, my child,
breathes the breath of winter's darkest day
everything contains its opposite
reckoning is today
have faith and wait
in the voice of silence
resides the dignity of speech
ships that have sunk in the sea
shall rise again as will the warriors slain
the tallest mountain crag
was once a level plain
do not weep for innocence, my child,
what was ever, is, remains the same
the wind unravels the Gordian knot of the brain
soothes the heat of the senses
and smooths the hollow bone
laurels won will be won again
and all defeats made sweet
do not weep my child
soon will come the snow
and then you'll sleep
and then you'll sleep.

Saying thus the wind passed away
into a whistling void between the sky and the sea
(and the snow came down
gentle as a mantle
over the fallen town).

CONEY ISLAND

Seeing myself distorted in mirrors
concave and convex
with the elongated torso of a giant
fingers like sticks
and the neck of an ostrich
or short and squat as a pregnant dwarf
with a head as broad and flat as a saucer,
I stick out my tongue
and move my limbs stiffly, one by one,
like a child
pulling the strings of a puppet.
The red light bulbs
make my face mottled
but knowing it's only pretense
and not an incurable disease
knowing it's only
knowing it's
only
I laugh
and one mouth is multiplied into many
all of the mirrors are laughing
the mirrors are filled with teeth as sharp as knives.

HOW HARD I TRIED TO REACH YOU
MY LITHE LITTLE BLOND SISTER

paddling frantic day and night
up rivers of the dark continent in a shaky canoe
without insurance
through waters thick with jawing crocodiles
hacking my way through dense underbrush
with my trusty machete sweat and a grin
TO KEEP ME COMPANY AMONG THE CANNIBALS

electric currents shooting slowly up your thighs
your brain flaming like a firecracker
the night tapping signals
a white ghost at your windowpane
the soft touch of ten strange fingers poised
intent upon your lips trying to understand
silent syllables formed upon your tongue

ringing numbers shrilly into silence
standing in rooms with seven empty hangers
hanging in the closet one for each day of the week
a cigarette smoldering in the ashtray
bedsheets crumpled
searching frantically through drawers
for a forwarding address
arguing with landlady bitches
who never received the rent
trailing you through clouds
picking up clues
storing them inside my head
a pack of cards to flip open at the opportune moment
snapping out
A ROYAL FLUSH TO WIN THE GAME
writing X-mas cards
returned a month later labeled **ADDRESS UNKNOWN.**

I am the girl
who walked two miles in the rain
at five one April morning
to catch tadpoles in the dark

shining a flashlight
the days flew past us so fast
we never knew
whether time was moving
or we were standing still
skipping giggles green bubblegum scribbles
on notes we crumpled into balls
and hurled across rooms
before the Rabbi thank God some secrets
still remain impenetrable as thorn hedges
my daughter's wide brown eyes her innocence
that dazzling sweet mysterious smile
which spells sex glowing red in the dark to touch
& hair that smells like cinnamon buns two dimples
I swear I will protect

How many times lugging heavy wornout luggage
tied with frayed rope climbing down
staircases in strange cities filled with fumes
and white ruins
I have called your name
only to have a stranger turn and coldly frown
your long-limbed grace
& shy-blue eyes signaling desperately
from a pale white face
on a moving train with semaphores flaring wildly
I pass you by
ten thousand miles between us in a wink

a silhouette in a window
watching flickering lights
waiting for footsteps which never come

BUT I AM COMING IF YOU ONLY WAIT

catching fireflies which glow in glass jars
swaying above us Japanese lanterns
in the long dusky summer nights
running after red salamanders which slither in and out
of the damp green moss under trees
& later lose their delicate spots and luster

triple-cheeseburgers wolfed down at lunch
followed by bags of salty chips

the boys from the camp on the opposite side of the lake
who watched us with telescopes
each time we skinny dipped
how I tried in vain to cover my breasts and leap
in quick
the way we hid
comic books under our bunks before **INSPECTION**
the wet leaves that trailed along the corridors
like tears the day they locked...

OR DID I IMAGINE ALL THIS.

How hard I tried to reach you my lithe little blond sister
locked at the top of the castle
you never wither
but continue to sing
high soprano in all weather

I am not good enough
I am the 'other'
the darker side who cannot shine
so this entire poem
is but a fragment of your song
as I walk through the rooms
in a house **TOO BIG TO BE REAL**
where talk is stuffed
there is one room filled with spears
which are really colored pencils
for me to take hold of
**THEY SHOW ME THE WAY OUT
OF THIS BLUEBEARD'S CASTLE**
in another room
a baby grand upon a pedestal waits and twirls
like a baton
how hard I tried to reach you
so your thin wrists might take hold of me
and firmly tell me
which one of us
the day the snow fell
and the doors closed behind with a final clang
sat laughing
a hyena
in excrement.

POEM FOR ELI BODI ENZER

They said you've got a tumor in your brain
and it's malignant
ma lig nant
even separating it into syllables can't make me understand
black
a beast
in the head of the great communicator of
light
a painter who never needed a canvas
for his words were paints
and his canvases
said something
words were quite inadequate.
For five nights
you talked in torrents
flying falling bursting in air like stalks of flames.
You said,"Don't let them bring my boy.
I want him somewhere where he's safe.
Tell him anything you want to,
but tell him in a place
where he's got all his things around him
things he knows.
Tell him slow and let it settle in.
I want him to remember me the way I was
not see his father that great golden giant
turn into a stinking hulk of rotten vegetable
babbling like an idiot.
Let him remember instead the stories
I told him at bedtime
of Victor Vulture, Marvin Moose,
David Bat, and Alan Alligator.
Let him remember the time we went camping
up at Moosehead Lake
when I chopped down that big tree for firewood."

Every few minutes you slurred your letters
forgot a word or syllable
and laughed in amazement to yourself
because you thought these things so clearly
and now everything was reduced to such simple truths

as clear as crystal in your head
only you couldn't find the word to show us where.

You cried out, "No.
Don't tell me the word.
I must try.
I am a communicator by profession
and an artist has to speak."

At night you could not sleep.
You thrashed about
like a wounded shark
and ground your teeth in anguish.
In the morning you said,
"It won't kill me if I can't ever speak again.
I can always paint.
I will paint great paintings.
I see them in my head."

When the telephone rang
it was this Senator from Mineola.
Hearing your voice boom back at him
in jest like you were sitting
in an office with a million typewriters going
clickety-clack
a business man on Wall Street
with a push-button phone
and two secretaries taking rapid dictation.

"There is a consciousness before and after
and forever
I see it all now,"
you suddenly said
after an hour of silence.
"Get that physicist friend of mine on the phone
if I can't talk when you reach him tell him
tell him
what I say
say that
I am passing from one level of awareness into another
I know it
I can feel it
tell him that I'm calm
that I'm not afraid.

Zim, when I get out of this,
we'll do wonderful things together
we'll have a house in the country
for our children
and we'll start this
business of ideas
two thousand dollars down for the idea
five thousand dollars down to put it into action
we'll be rich and fat
and sit in big houses laughing all day long.

You were still talking when the doctors came to take you in.
You turned to me and said,
"Tell my son that Marvin Moose is all right.
He's gone on a trip."

ST. MICHAEL'S CEMETERY

Lives I thought I had buried
leap alive tonight
an army of stone angels
strides forward
shields raised
against the dying light
wreaths of roses in their hair
stern flowers without scent.

On the other side of the iron fence
in St. Michael's
the dead
lie still without sense
bones shorn of pretense.

They do not dare to whisper there
where the mourners stand
a little band huddled together holding hands.
They buried grandpa
New Year's Eve
the night of the gravediggers' strike.
The moon opened wide as a cyclop's eye
while I fingered my rosary beads.

Death is a hex
a pain in the neck
don't laugh when you see
a hearse go by
hold your breath
or you may be
the next to die
death will get you in the night.
When You Least Expect It
lives in the cave
where all the dark things
chortle.
The girl of six began to whistle.

My heart is a dark season
of faded flowers. Why is it raining?

It is always raining here.
C'est une pays de la nuit,
the old woman said.
Her lover was dead.
Her words of love
were mouthed to the wind.
The taste on her tongue was bitter.

The graves are closer together now
visitors seldom come
except on Sundays
to deposit
those pallid bunches
of pitiful flowers
Tokens to
Tokens to
One
    for
        me
            and
One
   for
      you.

Somewhere
there's a man
chiseling a rock.

He is a maker of angels
Very busy.

He lives alone in a house of stone.
His heart is stone.
There are stone flowers in his garden
it is always cold there are no seasons.
I begin to shiver.

I too shall have
one stone angel
raise its passionless lips
to kiss the cool spring air.
Wreaths of roses in its hair.
At this very moment
it is
being
chiseled.

THE RED DEATH IS ALWAYS A SURPRISE

Monday on the other side of silence
sits a Cheshire cat
his eyes are slits which open
into worlds of black
sweet pretty kitty cat
who will not come
for milk and sugar
black Monday
black
the chimneys dark with dolor.

Tuesday no time hurry up now move along
with those white horses
bareback riders dressed in pink
and sequined smiles going thump thump thump
on the broad backs of dancing horses tossing roses
what we need here is a
short order
Circus Maximus
'cause Mr. Death's a bloody butcher
and I'd like to cut his heart out whole
stuff it down his throat
and watch him choke.

Wednesday I am sudden red
as a wounded fox running the brush in winter
dripping blood
chased by yapping hounds
and fierce-eyed hunter.

Friday you are dead.
"We mend everything but broken hearts"
the sign above the pawnshop said.

ALL ALONG THE HUDSON THE BOATS TOOT TONIGHT

to the bright moon
quiet as a Sphinx she winks
even with the windows closed
one can clearly hear them
call
they float in slow and black as shiny licorice sticks
their hulls lick the water smooth
spring rides into winter like a cowboy
on the wind frisky as a calico colt
which kicks its heels all silver
the deep scent of lilacs in the mist
drifts in from open sea
where sleep's a lavender kiss
love
knows
no such thing as distance
the halo dreams of children
are an always Christmas.

NIGHT JOURNEY

Here, a Houdini of the atmosphere
waves his staff and laughs
faces split in half like hearts
the depths of the sea part
incandescent fish
glide in the deep
by purple reefs
where lines criss-cross
loss
and open into blue forget-me-nots
at the edge of sleep
all clocks are stopped
houses stalk the hills like giant centipedes
and each spry hair supports a walking tree
see
life's a stage
where arrows point off the page
black hats cocked
the doors unlocked
people leap like acrobats
bright iridescent colors
alchemized to crystal
still waters murmur clear
calligraphic notes
which
tremble like a luminous cloud of letters
over buried cities
where the streets unravel into stairs
that lead nowhere
a feast of domes flags bells spires
rises higher
towards a red sun
floating like an eye
which winks in the pale dawn sky
come
cries the star of Bethlehem
it is not far
the moon swoons
soon
the unborn child
smiles.

BIRTH

A hand
is a fish
is a fetus
is a wish
is a smile
on the Nile
and a grinning
crocodile
the world a wild waste of water spinning
a dark black tunnel all funnel
blood curled in a bonnet
a green lilting sonnet
I push towards light
you cry
and I
lose the child I was
and become the mother I am.

AFTERNOON AT THE ZOO

I heard one otter say
to another
"Come
this is a back slapping the water day
and a rolling over to linger in sun
with flattened fins
and a long licking of water off whiskers."

We sit on the bench.
On the other side of the fence
wild Barbary Sheep
stare
their long curved horns
pierce the still air.

The Siberian Ibex
has a long red beard
silky and soft
he walks
on the balls of his toes
and leaps
like an acrobat.

White birds are walking on the frozen water.
Old men sit, heads pressed against the pane of glass.
They rub their hands together.

Did you ask why
flocks of birds
rose sudden and wild with beating wings
circled and swirled
to settle down amid the quiet reeds.

That woman with the leopard coat
headed towards the lions
she's in trouble.

HOMAGE TO KANDINSKY

As I walk the lonely miles
black lines are spears
which jut and thrust like night
Kandinsky's silver steeds gallop
through whirlwinds of ice
the north wind is a face
there are faces
everywhere
bright white lightning
in the moonlight of my eclipse
a laughing clown
clutches his belly
shakes like jelly
there are fishes in the sky
seas in the air
a man riding a white polar bear
each rock a carnivorous orange mouth
which greedily gulps the air
spires on the distant hills
rise like spider fingers
I
protest
in this *Garden of Love*
there are breasts without heads
facing dark blue streams
which run
towards
a red sun ringed in black like sorrow
going down
it sinks into the ground
without a sound
a ship without sails
sets out to sea
strange black insects
with tentacles like aerials
buzz questions
to a shape which floats in outer space
without a face
a note of music echoes
off the mountains like the teeth of sharks which tear
ladders lean on themselves

since houses have no doors or windows
the red sun is an eye which stares
red from weeping
everything is upside down
acrobats are in the air
camels have teats
that hang like cows
how
now
a circus
a festival of
and suddenly
it is summer
Little Pleasures
candycane and spices
red horses hot as peppers
pale pink clouds and suckling pigs
snakes that palpitate
like thighs
trills thrills
a yellow dragon beaming fire on the hills
a circus in the summer
a carnival in air
and everything is turned to green
(it seems a childhood dream)
green are the hills
green are the faces of the women
in their gossamer gowns
ripe is the fruit plucked from the bough
but the man in the black frock coat
is waiting
in the right-hand corner of the painting.

TRIBUTE TO ARSHILE GORKY

Gorky never needed to become Gorky
he was
tall lean and moustached
from the beginning
cosmological like the wandering Jew
who moved in from the out
hugging close like a cloak
to an inner dark and even desperation
hunched down inside
a ragged dream of light
bright broken
fragments spilled from arteries and veins
an ice skater cutting lines on canvas
in the dead of winter
fingers scratching hatching lines
like chickens in the spring like blood
like resurrection
bones these blades engraved in ice
blue on white
washes of red like rivers of running blood
bathed in golden light
doodling blind with lines like a dreaming child
he entered sight
a green deeper than hope
a forest of leaves richer than emeralds
breasts hanging from trees
branches like arms
banners waved in the sky
a marriage made in heaven
one solitary singing bird
squats obstinate on a charred and broken bough
how
man against nature
seeking
now
the perfect setting for a twentieth century
crucifixion
"To All My Loveds"
scrawled on the wall
everyone of us

All
hung with a noose
in an anguish of smoldering ochre.
Fall turned to fire
like a frenzied woman
swept the hills all black
Arshile Gorky
Come Back.

NOTE TO NOAH FROM HIS WIFE

Noah,
That day the night clouds swooped down,
vultures of darkness devoured the bloodred sun.

The rain started so slowly
nothing much
good for the grain
it hadn't rained much that March.

By five p.m. the fields were flooded.
"Enough," I thought and dozed, but
the sound of water splashed round
shook me from my sleep like endless tears
falling, beating on the walls.

I heard them, heard as you
hurried me towards the ark.
I never told you, Noah, but I
always thought you were crazy,
building a thing like that
right in the middle of the tomato patch.
But yes, I remember
counting
two by two
two elephants, two kangaroos——
two by two you said,
and Who were you to choose?
May I ask by what right,
by what staff your command?
I tell you
You and your damned animals,
"By order of Whom," I said and
I say it again.
Why you stood inside the ark,
didn't even see
the children running with outstretched arms,
the wave of water over the hill
like a gigantic arm and
screams and twisted limbs
falling through the air.

You and your damned animals
I say it again.

A wild waste of water
around us all ark and animals.
Why the stink was more than I could bear,
the rafters enclosed us, stifled us,
as the waters rose, willed to engulf
the earth and all living
but us-----
Oh
Noah
Why Us?

THE SCIENCE LESSON

On the blackboard
a paragraph
product of intelligence
neat, meticulous
granting limited information
in stages
the science lesson
progresses
week after week
a shrill voice echoes
in the room
the children sit.
David bends obedient.
Sylvia smiles her half smile
lacking intelligence
perceiving something
nevertheless.
Robert's pale blue eyes are
glazed.
He turns in his seat
slow as a tortoise
stunned
peers at a stuffed crane, breathes
the smell of mustiness.

In this room only
plants are green
facing towards the sun
sprout leaves.

Sylvia taps her fingers.
Isaac yawns.
The boy from Israel
giggles.
Pencils scribble.

The faces of these children
are blank
weary of much
endurance
is a

thing best known
by those
who can't even define it.

THE HIGH WIRE SPECIALISTS

Often women are clowns shot out of cannons
who leap out laughing
lie down
like mats.

But the best
are the high wire specialists.

Everyone has waited
for this act.
The wires
go up higher and higher
until they seem
invisible
and anyone crazy enough
to go up there
would have to freeze
or walk on air.

Still, out they come against all odds.
Stepping gently into the center ring,
they bow quietly.
Swift as gazelles they climb up
swaying rope ladders
with dainty red-painted nails
ribboned hair curled into soft ringlets
pink ballet shoes.

Suddenly
they are
standing on the narrow platform.
Breathless
balancing on a wire a mile above the gaping crowd.
No one dares make a sound.
Everyone stares.

How they manage to walk
is a process that can only occur
step by step
each move
a miracle.

Their secret specialty to live dangerously.
It was this they were bred for.

Eyes fixed on the sky like radar
lest they slip
to the ground.

STILL LIFE ARTIST

There, inside the garden
behind the wall,
the still life artist sits
preparing to paint a scene.

He has meticulously selected
and arranged
objects
he wishes us to see.

A trussed turkey.
A knife and fork.
A sharpened axe.
An elephant's ear.

And this could mean
could mean....

The shrubs
around the easel too
pruned and pared
into unnatural shapes

a dog that does not bark
a lark
with clipped wings
which cannot sing.

In their absolute precision
unreal.

He is waiting for the right moment
to pick up the brush
to capture a light
in the sky.
Meanwhile
the clock ticks.

On the other side of the wall
cypress trees

rise
forlorn spires in the dusk.

Imperfect in their beauteous flaws
they permit us (thank God)
to finally
breathe.

THE PHOTOGRAPH
for Stephen Michael

Certainly, there is something
I wish to keep
in this photograph
pinned over my desk
like a rare orchid
it has weathered the wiry onslaught
of two icy winters.

There it is always high noon
the middle of June
the sky, a perfect Robin's egg blue,
laced up neatly between the branches of oaks.
Pink roses clustered on the bush behind us
like mauve spotlights.

We stand   arms interlocked
legs outspread
football players
before the game
bowing to the crowd.

Our open smiles
deny spring fades
into the dry heat of summer.

Change is an impossibility
we take for granted like strawberries and cream
since we are lovers.
You, elephant head, about to burst out of my belly
your slow gorgeous blossoming reason enough for me
to be.

For once I do not need to ask questions
immune
proud as a gleaming Stradivarius
tuned and tuned to perfection.

The bunch of yellow daffodils I grasp tightly
in my fist
the lacy green ferns which trail along my slender wrist

cut from the stem
seconds before the snapshot
have begun to wither
a slight tinge of brown
stains the day around the edges.

THE WEDNESDAY LADIES

Wednesday is Ladies' Day
on the Long Island Railroad.

On Wednesday
the ladies
come into the city
to see the new exhibit at the Whitney.

In Pucci prints
alligator bags and shoes
lips half-opened chewing mints
they stare
at the paintings
toys stuffed into Christmas stockings.

They
devour the paint.

White gloves melt,
flowers wilt, and
voices like snakes curl in
to touch the outer limits of their lives.

The lecturer describes
the artist's struggles, and one
wonders
if she should have included
artichokes on the dinner menu.

AT THE EDGE OF THE DESERT

Waiting for the dawn's early light
after a sleepless night
the housewife
stands on the lawn
amid cacti calloused and bristly as hands
she holds a telescope up to the fading stars
as if to find....

Empty holes dug in the sand
from which nothing grows
black rubber hoses
coiled limp
venomous rattlers asleep
before the day's onslaught of heat.

Meaning runs off
easy as water in a dry season.

ENTERING ANOTHER COUNTRY

for Eli Bodi Enzer

Restless to fly off like Superman into another country
suddenly I see how all my countries
are countries of the mind which I traveled
like Marco Polo these thirty years.
What is stranger than what I am and what I make
of Balzac in his blindness
the woman leaning over the pool of water
watching drifting leaves the stares of strangers.
At sixteen sitting in my dream with long hair thrown casually
back over my shoulder wearing black leotards and tights
reading tea leaves in the garden of the Museum of Modern Art
in love with Will, the actor, whose keen
blue eyes like hawks winged into my life how he rode
all the way across the country traveling three days and nights
without sleep at seventy miles an hour in a derelict car
filled with half a ton of fresh picked apples and a case of
Rheingold
watching the sun rise in front and the moon set behind
the road a winding silver baton twirled by an invisible drum
                                 majorette
the high-pitched sound of tires humming
on the ground the whistling song of bees the day cracked wide
                                 open
split like a walnut another car flashing by quick as the speed of
                                 light
a wave then the story of how he crossed the Atlantic alone
in a boat. All stories of traveling
fascinated me early the points of connection with others
being the center of their dreams
and how I loved those most who came and went
the magicians and the sorcerers who left words in my mouth.

Always intrigued by those who managed to travel
to places I pored over
in the travel section of the *Times* on Sundays. Now I see
the countries I dreamed about can be entered by standing still.

To get to the center of a dream first you must learn to stand
absolutely still wherever you are and look in.

Turn three times to the south.
Turn once to the west. Place your hands upon your forehead.
                        Close your
eyes. Trust the prophets.

The postcards of paintings from Museums I began collecting
when I was fourteen
Grandma Moses scenes
miniature neat worlds that could be easily folded, placed
in a pocket, and carried everywhere to turn to and look at like
talismans.

The black glistening branches of tiny trees
lined on the horizon
flags waving madly in unison
white roaring streams churning power
like butter in a vat or vanilla ice cream
rolling frothy down steep green gorges
neat wooden planks keeping property
divided into separate plots
one for corn one for alfalfa one for brown and white cows
tiny trains green black red and gold
coal cars oil cars flat cars carrying yellow hay
white smoke signaling down long lengths of valleys
(clear signals everyone could know)
waterfalls where water fell clean starched white sheets
shaking out silver fishes
spilling down long hills
green meadows dotted with daisies where tiny white sheep
                        baahed and grazed
away long languid summer days.

(if there were only time enough to play)
under a red sun under a hot dry blue cloudless sky
teenagers sitting on the stoop of the ice cream parlor
drinking coca cola sipping ice cream sodas
through red and white striped straws
a red white and blue American flag
waving from the steeple of the one-room school house
where all the children black and white and yellow and brown
gather to learn useful things and read important books
filled with multi-colored three dimensional pictures
showing the way things should be
or were dreamed by other authors
the little yellow house with green shutters next to the creek

where a few gray geese honk in the yard
wash drying on the line
children playing a game of catch before dinner
men washing windows riding lawnmowers like stallions over the grass
standing at dusk chatting over fences after an honest day's work
long hoses sprinkling water like drops of mercury
on the parched mouths of the grass
pruning hedges with clippers into
squared off boxes
(no questions for which there are no answers)
always laughing children running in the woods
watching tadpoles change
into frogs
bagging fireflies
running home
when the red sun sinks slowly behind the horizon
like a friendly eye
and three bears snuggle down into a quilted bed
in a little tree-house filled with honey in the woods.

So much for Grandma Moses.
Suddenly I wake from my dream to discover I am thirty.
Halfway across the waters. Alone in the boat.
The house grows smaller and smaller
a child's vision of Christmas never includes
the roasting of the meat the baking of the bread
the hours of kneading
the hard work which goes on behind the scenes
in the bustling kitchen.
There is more to life than the bringing out of feasts
on platters. Than pictures.

There is the hoeing the mowing the raking the pruning the cleaning
the stripping the baking the steaming the turning the burning the
seaming.
I am the bread.
I am the meat.
I am the wool.
I am the hands.
I am the sheep.

Often, I stand in front of a painting by Rousseau which shows
a gypsy and a lion
because it is so still
because it is so still beneath the quiet swirling stars

white teeth glisten like pearls
fangs do not bite tan flesh.
There is no blood no snarl of anger there
I step into the painting's
starry air.
The man and the lion wait. They are familiar as my fingers.
The lion instead of tearing the man's dream asunder
lets him lie in his sacred kingdom of sleep
dreaming deep into the dream of whom he wishes he were
so wakening he can draw closer to all he can become.

Dreaming nightly of all the countries I must enter
dreaming of you, my friend, who are dead
who entered that strange country alone
I see labor is a death.
Women remain closest to the ground.
All things which decay
lie tainted with the pain of growth
pushing to enter a darker realm.
Sensitive as harps to the barely audible cries
heard in the depths of the jungle
the music of the whirling spheres
we must be birthed a second time perhaps a third
prepared for a new world with the births of our children
battered dragged drugged and bruised
run over by ten-ton trucks
we learn to ride it out by rocking with the pain.
In submitting we wait out the dark moist well
to burst forth at last in blood from tunnel into jagged light
inside the new peach skin of another self.
Changes are hard to endure.
Often persons cannot move at all for fear
but if we could not change we would all still be sitting in the
                                                        same
small room.

I open myself.
A clam's shell is pried open by a knife. It slips out. It is
boiled and eaten and it changes into something else.
I break the cord with my own teeth. Untie the knot with my
                                                       bleeding
thumb.
I lick out the dirt in the wound.
I peel open my skin.
Open to

become.

I watched a banana change. The flesh turned
dark and rancid. The inside grew soft and melted. The skin
spotted and rotted. Finally, the inside burst out.

Turning winding unwinding my dreams I split in a shower of sparks
a piece of meat on the spit gone through blue flames.
Everything seen does not encompass everything dreamed.
But what I dream is surely what I am and what I shall become.

I count my dreams like rosary beads.

Last night I entered China. Could not speak the language.
Somehow, God only knows how, we learn to communicate. The
                            day we
discover the foreigner is ourself it is essential to hand him
a glass of water and a crust of bread.

You are dead, my friend. You are dead.
The object of my love is gone.
That does not affect my ability to love.

Often these last ten years I dreamed of houses.
Fire tornadoes blizzards floods.
I could never escape.

Now I break open the door
step out.

Often, my friend, I remember those long scribbled barely
                            intelligible letters
you wrote from Hong Kong when you lived
on the top of the Peak during long green days filled with money
and cobras wiggling in the garden and strange-fruited sunsets like
ripe mangoes when Chinese gunboats in the harbour boomed
                          messages
all night long how you floated on those glowing islands of color
sailing the ship with sails outspread into the unknown holding hard
to the rudder into the center of a growing storm you never
faltered.

How it must be going toward death is the way it feels
that sudden stillness before the first pang of labor

never knowing before what it is you will enter or
if you will emerge intact
afterwards lying on your back you have come
swimming miraculously through seventy-foot high waves which
crushed you to bits drowned every bone broken somehow
cast on a sunlit shore safe and warm and still
you breathe.

In spite of my dreams of deadly worms which devour us
and cover the horizon like clouds
in spite of real earthworms which wiggle in the dirt beneath
                                          my feet
and will someday wiggle in and out of my own hollow skull

I can speak and say I am/ I will to be
I will change
            to become
                        what I am
                                    destined to be.

Wherever you are I send you my heart
                                    my tongue
                                              my teeth
                          and twelve gold fillings.

Like you I sleep and wake to enter another country.

RENDEZVOUS

Sitting among the *gazpacho* soups
today's special for twenty-one cents per bowl
and layers of double-frosted chocolate cake one-day old,
I listen to the sound of water spouting from the mouth
of a metal fountain
shaped like a deer
running through an artificial pool.

Surrounded by walls of stone
which shut out light
drinking tea for two I think of you
a thick gold bracelet on my arm
red-painted nails
you cannot see.

To this place paved of marble I have come
to be alone
during the hour of our rendezvous.
Only here inside this huge museum
floor above floor
stuffed with ancient relics
of broken lives preserved under glass
and the continuous sound of water running
do I feel safe
thinking how I have broken and mended before.

The newness of things outside frightens me.
Someday, among the faces which surround me,
smiles will become as singular as they are
your features fade out mercifully
like those of the Cheshire cat.
Meanwhile, I must stop pasting them over everything
a mad artist with a can of glue who cannot stop.
I must learn to talk to myself and listen
expect no one else to answer back.

Call this poem "Requiem for Winter" if you will.
Walking down cobbled paths
bare stiff branches
of trees waved overhead
a living awning

budding surely into
spring
sap racing rich through every swinging vein.

Only comfortable
surrounded by words pouring in and out like water
walls of words
words to sip like sugared tea
turning this way and that on Moving Day
searching for a still pool filled with lilies by which to sit.

When will I learn
such a place
cannot be found outside of art.

But if art is an illusion
nevertheless it helps us to survive.
It holds some measure of light. That cannot be denied.

This is the *Museum of Art.*
I live here. I never leave the premises.

I should have gone over to the *Chinese Calligraphy Section*
to puzzle out the beautifully drawn pictures of that foreign
         tongue.
To learn how to walk numb in a land without knowing the
         language.
To trust my senses amid bare branches where the moon is
         just
the moon and promises nothing else and there is finally an
         end to
symbols.

Turning this way and that on Moving Day.
Watching baggage piled outside your door.
Rooms I knew stripped down by strangers' hands
corpses emptied into sacks and carted off.

How can a painting showing a black and white floor
done by some minor Dutch painter of the seventeenth
         century
the way a rhododendron droops at four o'clock
a ray of light which shines through blinds on dusty leaves
fill me with such grief?

I carry this ability to juggle words
in order to go on without.
It is what one must have
when walls come tumbling down.

Take me away to a valley scourged by locusts
in some far-off summer
where the stripped trees and soured land
have begun to grow back.

Locked in this subterranean burial chamber
in a limestone sarcophagus
reached only by a perpendicular
shaft carved out of solid bedrock
at a depth of fifty-five feet I lie with severed arms
dreaming someday my prince will come.

Incurable romantic
what can you learn from a labyrinth without an end?
Do the remnants of Egyptian walls
give any indication of the living form within?

Learning
that hours move through days in spite of loss
would be a more profitable occupation.

Still I am committed to shining lights
in the eyes of a blindman.

THE HOUSE IN THE WOODS

All afternoon I sit as still as a log
my senses numb
waiting for you to come.
In the sun of dragonflies
white cumulous clouds rise and fall
like breath in the mouth of a gentle God.
"Waiting for my echo, my shadow."

Yesterday, the dragonflies emerged from the pond
singly then in swarms.
Today blue iridescent wings
brush my cheek.
Gentle soaring acrobats
whose antics
make me laugh.

The rye grass I planted sprouts so fast.
Everyday something in the woods has changed.
One day hepatica's bright blue
the next, yellow daisies with black eyes.
Pink dogwood
a crazy froth laced trunks of trees
now not a single trace
of velvet petals remains.

Living on the land teaches
the invalidity of asking why and when.
I have much to learn from nature
concerning patience.
I lived too long
in a city
where words
were the only woods to enter
and I planted, pruned, bulldozed
at will.

All afternoon I sit as still as a log
my senses numb
in the sun of dragonflies
waiting for you to come.

Love's not built on logic
a mystery whose secret can be easily unlocked.
I am not a mechanic.

Dusk comes instead of you.
The brook rushes past my door. I step
into churning foam
washing downstream lightly as a leaf
tossed between high granite rocks.
Leaving grief
I sail into a new country
where love drips like honey on everyone's tongue
and the inhabitants have never heard of thieves.

Here, I begin to forget myself.
Isn't this what I always wanted
to live alone in a house in the woods
doors flung open
locks broken?
This says something too
about love   how it remains open.

Of course you have not come.
I am telling this story
to myself. The woods walk in.
First, red oaks, those proud statesmen.
Then, maples, firs and beech.
I must let go of adjectives.
To learn to speak strip down to nouns.
A silver birch bent double
from gale winds
presents a leathery bark which says
"Here I am. I offer no explanation
though you are perfectly free to question."

"Just close your eyes
I'll be there anytime."

Silence
the challenge
forces conjecture.

Here, new graves are planted
at the head with sticks
upon which

names are fixed
on white slips
of paper.
Strange seeds wait to burst
into flower in spring showers.

Another woman's head
lies cradled on your pillow.
She possesses you even while you sleep
takes you for granted
like vitamin pills.

But I speak of love.
I am stubborn.
I repeat the same words over and over.

      I am a displaced person
      looking nightly
      for a house
      I have only seen in dreams
      a house whose structure
      made of a magic unknown element
      can never be broken into dust
                              like stone
    melted into water
             like ice
    burned into ash
           like wood

alone
from ashes I come
trailing long dark lashes over bleeding wounds
dangling golden charms
singing tunes
a crazy gypsy under the moon
under the full moon in whose path I walk a proud white swan
under the crescent moon
a gypsy whose tent vanishes
before the morning sun
always the outcast   the wanderer
waiting for the mountain to fall the sign to appear in flames
swinging buckets filled to the brim
with dreams
which slosh onto the floor

stars shining in puddles
moons carried about like silver stones in secret pockets.

LETTING GO

Letting go of a dream
is going into the transitional stage of labor
suddenly
without preparation
no time to eat jello.

No anesthesia takes effect.
Nothing said in advance
could have told you
what it was like

to live through
and come out.

It remains
a second skin you cannot quite peel off.
Hurts when touched in the wrong spot
a wound that clots
but does not scar and heal.

A hole in the center of each day
you waken unwilling to face
are forced to skirt around
like a blind man tapping with a stick.

Fumbling everywhere
a long long time
for walls
you held onto.

HERE THEY COME THE MARCHING DRUMS

with a ra tat tat
and a ra ta tat tat
Snare Kettle Base.
A Jingling Johnny
carried aloft by marching bands
during the Austro-Turkish Wars
followed closely
by three
military
U.S. Infantry Drums that never lack for use
thump thump thump
the pieces of bodies
slide into plastic bags tied up like fruit
shipped back to the States first class
for the families to bury
painted
with stars and stripes
the eagle
claws outspread
clutches
thirteen leaves of grief
thirteen poison arrows
crowned
with blazing
thorns.

Here they come
down the street
on the Fourth of July. Ribboned in red blue and white.
Watch the children cry with delight.
With a ra tat tat tat
and a ra ta tat tat
Snare Kettle Base
Jingling Johnny
U.S. Infantry Drums
followed closely by
bombs dropped like flakes of snow in flickering light
on rice paddies
leaving dead mothers curled like leaves
eyeless babies

whose skins peel off as easy as layers of onions.

Here come the marching drums.

LESSON OF THE HORN IN G

Standing alone in a gray-carpeted room
breathing silence
I examine a white porcelain horn
drawn
with blue apple blossoms and lemon leaves
like Delft tile
too fragile to have ever been
intended for practical use
never meant to witness
the flash of hooves hitting the dust
along the winding paths of sunset
where the gray fox darts in terror
by bloodhounds
cornered in the center of a dancing circle
of strangers
shot
limp
drenched with blood.

The delicate blossoms and leaves
tell us the artist
wanted the spectator centuries later
to stop and wonder
for what earthly use
such an incredible instrument was made.

One invents the circumstance to fit the music.

Impossible instrument of beauty
love
seen at a distance   imagined
ruinously
shattered
by the first
note.

Still, silence leads to questions.

I paste a label on the glass case.

It reads: Horn of Silence
          Intended for Poets and Angels.

THEMES WRITTEN UNDER STRESS

I arrive at a place without churches or priests
and dream of constructing a powerful horse.
Dark brown.
His nostrils flare.
I ride him bareback in the moonlight
by the shining water
muscles rippling like water.

Looking through the lens of the eyes
to record things outside
which never match the inner vision.
Disparity between what is seen and what is dreamed.
A jigsaw puzzle with pieces missing.

The sky cannot fail
since it is always there.

One cannot accept knowledge
for which one is not
prepared.

When parts of the cerebral cortex
are stimulated by electrodes
the subject of the experiment
recalls
a specific scene
and relives the emotions connected to it.

The brain as a warehouse
in which we wander.
A needle stuck in a groove of a record
played over and over.

We break ourselves in pieces
to piece ourselves together.

To walk through flames
and still have faith
the mark
of the true believer.

Everything is a matter of perspective.
The shadows cast by the poplar trees
on the East Side Drive
are long in the morning
short in the afternoon.
They inch slowly from left to right
as the sun moves through its arc in the sky.

Sun and moon.
Opposite sides of the same face.
Without the sun
there would be no shadows.

Cars rush through
striations of darkness and light.
The drivers bent over wheels
do not see
leaves trembling
in the offshore breeze.

When I first flew in an airplane
I was amazed to see
a world of pattern
I never knew existed.

I must persist
to reach an order of which
I am at present unaware.
The only clue is pain.
The mind breaks a circuit
to form a new connection.

Tuning up the tired chambers of the heart
like a loose violin string
in order to play a particular tune
will not do...will not due.

What you choose
is who you are.

Each of us riding around
in a self-contained
vehicle
lost in the sunken chambers of the heart
a Nautilus.

The poet
searching for the word to fit the thought
sifts words like grains of sand.
Believing
he will
find the perfect instrument
to express the inner music.

One must accept a broken string.

The vessels of the body
arteries, cells, veins
obedient soldiers
carrying out
messages imprinted in genes.

Unutterable hours, months, years
locked in hotel rooms
under glaring bulbs
with a stale glass of water
and butts of cigarettes
in London in Paris
composing imaginary letters
to a lost lover.

Even our fictions
explain us.

How futile
to expect a prince to come
after one has bolted the gate
locked the doors
hidden the key
cut the wire to the telephone.

The moment
he hands over the key
the poet retreats to forge another
in the swirling waters of the sea.

Dreams tell us
how to cross
the dark waters
alone in the boat
without oars.

Night has fallen.
The lights on shore fade out.

A clamshell dropped by a seagull
splits open on a rock.

Eyes tell meanings
words cannot.

The smallest physical gesture
reveals intention.

To think of love.
Of what it is.
How often it is made of need.
To love the person
not one's idea of the person.

Smashing the walls of the body
to enter another's
one finds oneself
a stranger in a foreign country
who has yet to learn an adequate language.

Our only language
ourselves.

RIVER POEM

The entire river can never be seen
by one man
sitting on a windowsill.

We grasp
only part of the whole.
What we see
depends
upon position.

Today, a lady dressed in blue
leans on the iron railing
by the bank of the river.

For five days
she has stood there
at the same spot
looked up to watch
the faces of patients
at Payne Whitney Psychiatric Clinic.

She stares intensely. Waiting.
I want to tell her
not to leap.

I open the window as far as I can.

We have reached
the same place
though she is outside
and I am locked in.

Can one never see another
except through
a distorted lens?

This conjecture
may be utterly false
and she merely
waiting for a lover but I doubt it.

The vital things we say
are not in words but gestures.

I lean far out the window
waving wildly
the way sailors do
when two ships
pass
at night
on a rough sea.

There are hidden currents.
The tide turns quickly treacherous.
A long way
to reach calm waters.

Holding
bright jagged
fragments of our lives
like talismans.

Water
moves
of its own volition.

The woman in blue
motions with her arms
for me to come down.

I shake my head soundlessly.
She walks away
slowly kicking stones.

I am left alone
with the river.
It is very still.

Wanting to be a white seagull.
Wanting to move
in accordance
with a deeper natural rhythm.
Without thought.

But even the river
does not flow

in unbroken solitude.

Tankers carrying oil
red tugboats
barges filled with sand cement and coal
plow through
leaving in their wake
huge waves of white foam
which gradually subside
splash on rocks.

Once touched
forever altered
by memory
and expectation.

THE SIMPLE THINGS

You should have all the oranges you want to eat
and plenty of books to read.
A bed.
A desk.
A chair.
How nice your window overlooks the garden.
Did you hear me whistle from the other
side of the wall?

Tell me how your days go
show me each place
so I can picture you there.
Pick up the baby.
She wants to see the river too.
She speaks whole sentences
perfectly now.
Yesterday, she said to me,
"Mommy come back soon?"

www.ingramcontent.com/pod-product-compliance
Lightning Source LLC
Chambersburg PA
CBHW031419040426
42444CB00005B/639